McDougal, Littell

Handwriting 2

Connections 2

Houghton Mifflin Company   Boston
Atlanta   Dallas   Geneva, Ilinois   Palo Alto   Princeton

Consultants

The following educators reviewed lessons during the development of the *Handwriting Connections* program.

Bettye S. Anderson, Teacher, Crestline Elementary School, Mountain Brook, Alabama

Lawrence Barretto, Teacher, Maplewood Elementary School, Coral Springs, Florida

Ruth Black, Curriculum Assistant for Writing; Chairperson, District 39 Language Arts Curriculum Review Committee; Wilmette Junior High School, Wilmette, Illinois

Mary K. Butcher, Teacher, Thomas Edison Elementary School, Port Huron, Michigan

Dr. Hazel S. Harvey, Elementary Curriculum Supervisor, Hillsborough County Schools, Tampa, Florida; Adjunct Professor, Nova University, Ft. Lauderdale, Florida

Sr. Paul Mary Janssens, O.P., Principal, St. Edward School, Chicago, Illinois

Nancy R. Lancaster, Language Arts Specialist, Escondido Union School District, Escondido, California

Phyllis M. Rantz, Principal, John E. Burke School, Peabody, Massachusetts

Christine Robertson, Principal, Bramble Elementary School, Cincinnati, Ohio

Ophelia Q. Smith, Teacher, J. J. Rhoads Elementary School, Houston, Texas

Debra Smith-Sokolowsky, Teacher, Kennedy Elementary School, Succasunna, New Jersey

Blossom Blackman Stobb, Grade-Level Chairman, Oak Meadow Elementary School, North East Independent School District, San Antonio, Texas

Dahlia Tesher, Teacher, Jensen Scholastic Academy, Chicago, Illinois

Florence Viola, Teacher, St. Michael the Archangel School, Levittown, Pennsylvania

Multicultural Advisory Committee

Andrea B. Bermúdez, Professor of Multicultural Education; Director, Research Center for Language and Culture; University of Houston—Clear Lake

Martha Garland Livisay, Curriculum Specialist in Multiethnic Education, Ann Arbor, Michigan

Special Contributors

Design Concepts
Design 5, New York, New York

Covers
Ryan Roessler, Cover Photography

Acknowledgments

Isabel Joshlin Glaser: "Writing on the Chalkboard" by Isabel Joshlin Glaser, from *More Surprises,* Harper & Row, 1987. The author controls all rights.

Illustrations and Photography

Commissioned
Angela Adams: **44-46, 142, 145-148, 150;** Dave Albers: **81;** Yvette Banek: *ur* **25, 110;** Lisa Berrett: **56, 57;** Delana Bettoli: **60, 136, 137;** Steve Bourgeois: **17;** Katy Bratun: **86, 98, 99;** Stephanie Britt: **124, 125;** Nan Brooks: **27, 120, 121, 130, 131;** Rebecca D. Brown: *b* **1, 8, 10,** *b,* **11, 16, 17, 28, 33, 36 37, 49, 59, 63,** *b* **76, 77-79, 117,** *fr* **121, 141, 153, 154;** Ralph J. Brunke: **3, 4, 5, 22, 23,** *ur* **33, 47, 53, 92, 93, 96, 100, 111, 118, 122, 123, 126, 127, 139;** Brian Cody: **54, 55;** Jean Helmer Cassels: *b* **18, 19;** David Cunningham: **35, 115;** Mike Dooling: *br* **8, 9;** Malcolm Farley: **94, 95;** T R Garcia: **2, 62, 138, 155;** Robert Giusti: **35;** Paul Harvey: **58, 84, 85;** Steve Henry: **89, 108;** Brian Karas: **11, 153;** Carl Kock: **82, 83, 101;** Benton Mahon: **80, 97;** Susan Nethery: **40, 41, 43;** Sharron O'Neil: **38, 39, 87, 143, 149;** Dana Regan: *ur* **30, 31, 36;** Bruce Sereta: **6, 7, 10, 66, 67, 77;** Jerry Smath: **29, 36, 49, 61, 72, 73, 91, 103, 116, 119, 141, 154;** Susan Swan: *all ul* **18-21, 24-27, 30-33, 38-41, 44-46, 50-53, 56, 57, 80-89, 92-95, 98-101, 104-107, 110-113, 118-127, 132-139, 142-144, 146-149;** Peggy Tagel: **17, 52, 64, 65, 117, 152;** George Ulhrich: *c* **76;** Robert Voights: **23, 28, 90, 102;** Rhonda Voo: **14, 15, 133-135;** John Wallner: **74, 75**

Stock Photography
1: © Jeffrey Cadge/The Image Bank; **17:** Steve Bourgeois; **20:** *ur* © John Gerlach/Tom Stack & Associates; **21:** *ur* © John Gerlach/Tom Stack & Associates; **22:** *lr* © Manuel Rodriguez/The Image Bank; **26:** *ll* © Tony Freeman/ Photo Edit; **27:** *ur* © Tony Freeman/Photo Edit; **37:** © Werner Bokelberg/The Image Bank; **50:** Thomas Hovland/Grant Heilman Photography; **51:** © Ron Kimball; **63:** ©1987 Chris Springmann/The Stock Market; **79:** © LaFOTO/H. Armstrong Roberts; **81:** © Moos/Hake-Greenberg/Peter Arnold, Inc.; **88:** © Frank Oberle/Photo Researchers, Inc.; **104, 105, 106, 107:** NASA; **112:** C. Bryant/H. Armstrong Roberts; **113:** ©1990 Mark E. Gibson; **117:** © Elyse Lewin/The Image Bank; **132:** © Nik Wheeler/ West Light.

ISBN-13: 978-0-8123-7696-8   ISBN-10: 0-8123-7696-X

1998 Impression
Copyright © 1993 McDougal, Littell & Company
All rights reserved. Printed in the United States of America

C ontents

UNIT 4 Getting Ready to Write Cursive 63

UNIT 5 Writing to Learn *Handwriting Focus: Spacing and Slant* 79

UNIT 6 Writing to Celebrate *Handwriting Focus: Smoothness* 117

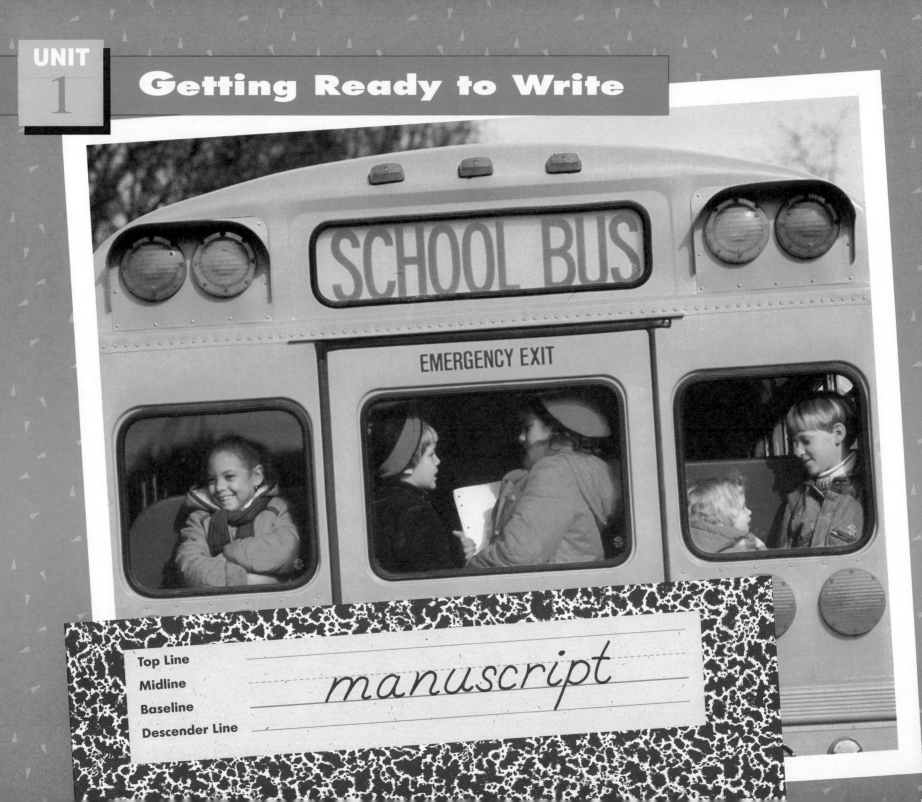

Top Line	
Midline	*manuscript*
Baseline	
Descender Line	

Read the poem "Writing on the Chalkboard" by Isabel Joshlin Glaser.

Writing on the Chalkboard

Up and down, my chalk goes.
Squeak, squeak, squeak!
Hush, chalk.
Don't squawk.
Talk softly when you speak.

Copy the poem on page 2, beginning
with the title. Use your best handwriting.

Letters can be made to look different.
Here is how the letters might look in the books you read.

Make a finger puppet.

This is how you would write the same sentence.

Make a finger puppet.

Tell how the letters are different.

A a   B b   C c   D d

E e   F f   G g   H h

I i   J j   K k   L l

M m   N n   O o   P p

Q q   R r   S s   T t

U u   V v   W w   X x

Y y   Z z

Sit tall.
Keep both feet
on the floor.

Slant your paper like this.
Hold your paper steady with your right hand.

Look at the picture.
Then look at the
way you hold your
pencil. Do not hold
your pencil too
tightly.

6

Right-handed Writers

Slant your paper like this.
Hold your paper steady
with your left hand.

Sit tall.
Keep both feet
on the floor.

Look at the picture.
Then look at the
way you hold your
pencil. Do not hold
your pencil too
tightly.

7

Letter Shape

When letters are shaped correctly, words are easy to read.
Close up any ovals in letters like **a, g,** and **o.**

kangaroo   **NOT** kunyuroo

Cross **t**'s and **f**'s.

flutter   **NOT** fluller

Dot **i**'s and **j**'s.

juice   **NOT** juice

Tell what words are easy to read.

terrific   jum   end

Letter Size

These are the names of the lines on which letters are written.

Top Line

Midline

Baseline

Descender Line

These letters touch the top line.

b d f h k l t

These letters touch the midline.

a c e i m n o r s u v w x z

These letters reach down below the baseline to the descender line.

g j p q y

Tell what word has letters three different sizes.

rain   tag   blocks

9

Letter and Word Spacing

Leave the space of a pencil point between letters.

octopus

Leave the space of a pencil between words.

a ship

Leave a finger space between sentences.

Come on! Swim with us.

Space letters evenly. Your writing will look better if you do.

Correct Spacing

my friend

Incorrect Spacing

mygo ldf i sh

These are straight.

rockets

These are slanted.

globes

All your letters should slant in the same direction.

The spaceship landed.

Your letters should look smooth.
Smooth letters are easy to read.

Correct

space

Too dark

space

Too shaky

space

11

Write your numerals carefully.

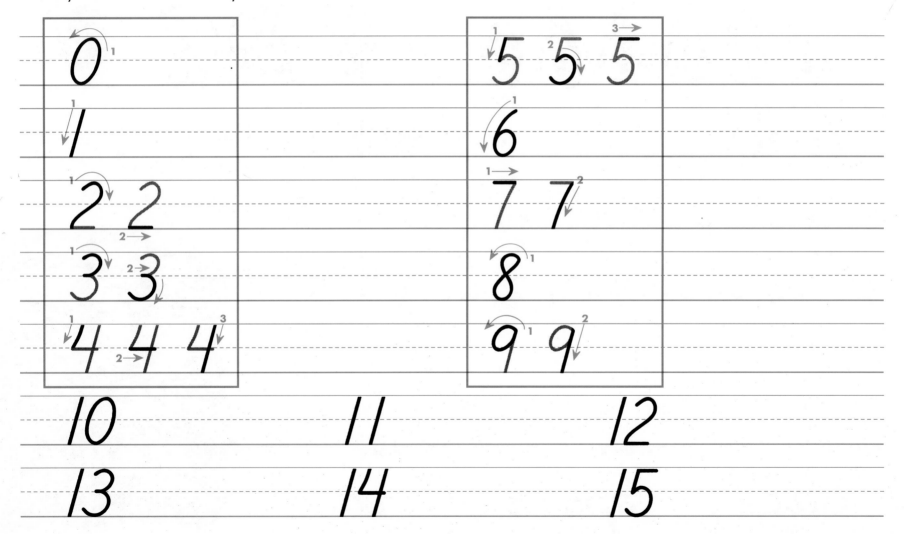

Copy each of these problems. Write every numeral in the right place.

$$7 + 8 = 15 \qquad 2 + 4 = 6$$

$$+ \qquad = \qquad + \qquad =$$

$$3 + 6 = 9 \qquad 7 + 5 = 12$$

$$+ \qquad = \qquad + \qquad =$$

$$\begin{array}{r} 15 \\ +3 \\ \hline 18 \end{array} \qquad + \qquad\qquad \begin{array}{r} 13 \\ +4 \\ \hline 17 \end{array} \qquad +$$

The Period

A sentence that tells something is a **statement**. Use a period at the end of every statement.

Rafael collects rocks.

I collect stickers.

Some words can be written in a shorter form called an **abbreviation**. Use a period after an abbreviation.

Monday   Mon.

Street   St.

14   **ON YOUR OWN**   Write a statement that tells something about you.

The Question Mark

A sentence that asks something is a **question**.
Use a question mark at the end of a question.

? _ _ _ _ _ ? _ _ _ _ ?

Did you meet my puppy?

Can you count his spots?

Is Wags a good name?

SELF CHECK   Circle the question mark you wrote at the end of each question.

15

Tell which letter has the correct shape.

_b_   _q_

Tell which letters reach down below the baseline.

_y_   _t_   _p_   _e_

Rewrite the sentence with the correct spacing.

Ise eyo u.

Write the word so that the letters slant in the same direction.

pretend

Write this word smoothly.

aquarium

October 14

Dear Diary,

Today I caught a huge grasshopper!

a
A

a   a
A   A   A

a   a   a
A   A   A

anthill   crawling ants

Ants are all around.

18 **SELF CHECK** Circle your best A.

b

B

b b

B B

b

B

best bug

Become a Bug Club member.

Be a buddy to a bug.

ON YOUR OWN   Write a sentence that describes your favorite bug.

19

c
C

c
C

c _ _ _ _ _ _ _ c _ _ _ _ _ _ _ c
C _ _ _ _ _ _ C _ _ _ _ _ _ C

cocoon

Carlos collects caterpillars.

Carlos colecciona gusanos.

20 ★ **ON YOUR OWN** Write a sentence that tells what you collect or would like to collect.

d   d   d
D   D   D

different

Dragonflies are slender.

Daddy-longlegs are speedy.

ASK A FRIEND Have a friend circle your best d.

21

Linking Handwriting to Writing

Writing a Diary Entry

Read this entry from a Bug Club member's diary.

September 19

Dear Diary,
I went to my first
Bug Club meeting. I
showed my cricket,
Chirpy, to the other
members.

22   💻 COMPUTER TIP   When you complete a sentence, press the space bar two times after the punctuation.

Copy the diary entry.

September 19

e

E

e   *e*   e

E   E   E

everyone   here

Eva's family had a barbecue.

They enjoyed being together.

24   ★ **ON YOUR OWN**   What do you and your relatives like to do together? Write about it.

f

F

f   f   f

F   F   F

Fernández family

Aunt Fran   Uncle Jeff

from Florida

Writing Connection: Telephone List
Theme: Family Reunion

ASK A FRIEND Have a friend circle an *f* or *F* that you need to improve.

25

g
G

g g
G G

g _ _ _ _ _ _ _ _ g _ _ _ _ _ _ g
G _ _ _ _ _ _ _ _ G _ _ _ _ _ _ G

Grown-ups gave lots of hugs.

Great-grandpa got hugs.

26 ★ **SELF CHECK**   Circle a *g* that touches the descender line.

h

H

h   h   h

H   H   H

home   reach

Hillary and Eva promised

to phone each other.

Writing a Telephone List

Copy what Eva wrote in a family telephone book she made.

F   *Fernández*   *Fernández*   **F**

Hector
(713) 555-1912
Hillary
(419) 555-1621
Leah
(312) 555-4811

ON YOUR OWN Make a list of the family members you call often. Put their names in alphabetical order.

Eva's cousin Sam helped out at the barbecue.
Copy his list of things to do.
Watch the sizes of your letters as you write.

1. Fill cups with milk.
2. Choose fruit for dessert.
3. Help do the dishes.

Circle the letter you wrote best.

Circle a word in which all the letters are the correct size.

29

i

I

i   *i*

I   *I*   *I*

i _ _ _ _ _ *i* _ _ _ _ _ *i*

I _ _ _ _ _ *I* _ _ _ _ _ *I*

invite   invitar

Iris will camp in her yard.

Iris will invite friends.

30   ★ **SELF CHECK**   Circle your best *i* 's.

j
J

j j j
J J J

juice   el jugo

Jan's job is to make juice.

Jan enjoys camping.

ON YOUR OWN   Draw something you like to do. Write a sentence about your picture.

31

k   k   k

K   K   K

k _ _ _ _ _ _ k _ _ _ _ _ _ k

K _ _ _ _ _ _ K _ _ _ _ _ K

keep   guardar

Kim is taking her knapsack.

Kim likes to pack quickly.

ON YOUR OWN   Write a sentence that tells what you think is in Kim's knapsack.

l   *l*

L   *L*

l   *l*   *l*

L   *L*   *L*

list   *la lista*

Luis will make a checklist.

Luis will write carefully.

ASK A FRIEND   Have a friend circle your best *L* .

Checklist
1. tent
2. first-aid kit
3. trail mix
4. jackets

33

Linking Handwriting to Writing

Writing a Checklist

Copy Luis's checklist of things for camping.

Checklist
1. tent
2. first-aid
kit
3. trail mix
4. jackets

ON YOUR OWN   Imagine you could camp out on the moon. What would you take?

Anansi and Tiger

What if Snake had escaped before Anansi could finish tying him to the bamboo? Write a new ending for the tale. Tell another way Anansi could catch Snake.

Iris has plans for a day at camp.
Copy this part of her schedule.
Watch the size of your letters as you write.

1:30   Hike to the lake.
2:30   Look for birds.
3:30   Decorate T-shirts.

Circle the capital letter you wrote best.

Circle a word in which all the letters are the correct size.

My Blue Kite
My blue kite
soars high up
to the sky.

m
M

m *m* *m*
M M M M

m _ _ _ _ _ _ m _ _ _ _ _ _ m

M _ _ _ _ _ _ M _ _ _ _ _ _ M

Mimi   monkey

Make-believe animals may

seem almost human.

SELF CHECK Circle your best *m*.

n

N

n _ _ _ _ _ n _ _ _ _ _ n

N _ _ _ _ _ N _ _ _ _ _ N

nosy elephant

My name is Neil Elephant.

Mi nombre es Neil Elefante.

o
O

o   o   o

O   O   O

Olga Owl
Owls in stories are
often old and wise.

40   ⭐ **ASK A FRIEND**   Have a friend circle an O that is closed.

p p p p p p

p p p p p

porcupine

Percy is unhappy.

Perhaps Olga can help.

ON YOUR OWN Write a sentence that a storybook animal might say.

41

Linking Handwriting to Writing

Writing a Story

Proofreading Read the story below. Tell what proofreading marks are needed to correct capital letters and periods.

Proofreading Marks

≡ Use a capital letter. <u>ted</u>.

⊙ Add a period. Go now⊙

Percy Porcupine was sad. no one could hug him. He had sharp quills One day his friends came to help. olga Owl had an idea

Final Draft Copy the story. Make the corrections
that your proofreading marks show.

HANDWRITING TIP Remember to close all your *o*'s and O's.

_____

- -

_____

- -

_____

- -

_____

- -

_____

- -

_____

ON YOUR OWN Finish the story. Tell what you think Olga Owl's idea is.

q
Q

q   q
Q   Q

q   q   q
Q   Q   Q

Queen Quail

Quiet! The queen will
settle a quarrel.

⭐ **ASK A FRIEND**   Have a friend circle any *q* that needs to be made better because it looks like a *g*.

r
R

r   r
R   R   R

r _ _ _ _ _ _ _ r _ _ _ _ _ _ _ r

R _ _ _ _ _ _ _ R _ _ _ _ _ _ _ R

read parts

Roberto will play a rude

rabbit named Rufus.

ON YOUR OWN   Write a sentence telling what problem a rude rabbit might have.

45

s

S

s

S

s   s

S   S

a snake

Sara plays a smart snake.

She hisses as she speaks.

★ **ON YOUR OWN**   Make a list of other words that describe a snake.

t
T

t   t   t
T   T   T

timid tiger
Tell Titus to talk
very softly.

SELF CHECK Circle a *t* that touches the top line and is crossed.

Linking Handwriting to Writing

Writing a Play

Copy these lines from a story that is written as a play.
Be sure to write the names of the characters.

Queen.   *What's wrong?*

Snake.   *Rufus hides things!*

Tiger.   *Tell him to quit.*

ON YOUR OWN

Write a sentence telling what Rufus might say. Then write a sentence telling how the problem with Rufus might be solved.

Copy the beginning of the story "The Shoemaker and the Elves." Try to shape each letter correctly.

Quite a long time ago, a shoemaker had leather for only one pair of shoes.

Circle the letter you wrote best.

Circle a word you wrote that has all the letters shaped correctly.

u *u* *u*

U *U* *U*

u _ _ _ _ _ _ *u* _ _ _ _ _ _ *u*

U _ _ _ _ _ _ *U* _ _ _ _ _ _ *U*

munch   quack

Animal sounds are fun.

Use them in your poems.

50 ⭐ **ON YOUR OWN**   Make a list of animals and the sounds each one makes.

V
V

V   V   V

V   V   V

Velvet

Lively eyes,

Silver fur,

Very soft,

I love her.

SELF CHECK Circle your best *V* and *V*.

51

w w w

W W W W

w _ _ _ _ _ w _ _ _ _ _ w

W _ _ _ _ _ W _ _ _ _ _ W

Write words that rhyme.

dragon wagon

slow crow

pale whale

ON YOUR OWN Make a list of words that rhyme with way.

x

X

x _ _ _ _ _ _ x _ _ _ _ _ x

X _ _ _ _ X _ _ _ _ X

Xavier's poem

Max, a boy,
has a toy.
It's a fox
in a box!

Linking Handwriting to Writing

Writing a Poem

Copy the title, the author's name, and the four lines of "The Little Turtle" on the next page. As you write, use words in place of the pictures. Look at the Word Box to find the words you need.

The Little Turtle

by Vachel Lindsay

There was a little .

He lived in a .

He swam in a .

He climbed on the .

WORD BOX

box   puddle   rocks   turtle

ON YOUR OWN   Think of other words that rhyme with *box*. Write a new last line for the poem.

55

y
y

y y
y y

y y y

yummy honey

Furry Bear loves honey.

You may like honey, too.

SELF CHECK Circle your best y and Y.

z

Z

z _ _ _ _ _ z _ _ _ _ _ z

Z _ _ _ _ Z _ _ _ _ Z

zooms   buzzes

Zippy Bee zooms and buzzes.

Zippy likes to save his honey.

Linking Handwriting to Writing

Writing a Cartoon

Look at the cartoon below and at the three words in the box.
Write the word that should go in each cartoon balloon.

Yeow!   Yum!   Buzz.

ON YOUR OWN   Draw pictures to show what happens next. Write words to tell what the bear and the bee say.

Sometimes handwriting is not easy to read. You can improve your handwriting by learning the reasons for handwriting problems.

Causes of Handwriting Problems

1. not closing letters

    jacket

    jacket

2. closing looped letters

    idgi

    edge

3. creating loops in letters with no loops

    qeeickly

    quickly

4. using straight strokes instead of round ones

    camper

    camper

Write this sentence in your best handwriting. Keep the handwriting problems in mind as you check your work.

Look at the bear.

The Three Billy Goats Gruff

Pretend you are a reporter who interviews the Three Billy Goats Gruff after they have crossed the bridge. Write a question for one of the billy goats. Then write the goat's answer.

60

Copy the English version or the Spanish version
of this poem, "Beautiful Butterfly."
Try to shape each letter correctly.

English
Shining butterfly,
Butterfly of pure gold,
On its wings a treasure,
Flying butterfly.

Spanish
Mariposa luminosa,
Mariposa de puro oro,
En las alas un tesoro,
Mariposa voladora.

Circle your best letter.

Circle a word you wrote that has all the letters shaped correctly.

61

Copy the poem "Writing on the Chalkboard" by Isabel Joshlin Glaser on your own paper. Begin with the title. Use your best handwriting.

Writing on the Chalkboard

Up and down, my chalk goes.

Squeak, squeak, squeak!

Hush, chalk.

Don't squawk.

Talk softly when you speak.

Cursive is fun!

Cursive is fun!

Two Alphabets

How are the letters in each pair alike? How are they different?

a a   b b   c c   d d

e e   f f   g g   h h

i i   j j   k k   l l

m m   n n   o o   p p

q q   r r   s s   t t

u u   v v   w w   x x

y y   z z

Two Alphabets

A A B B C C D D
E E F F G G H H
I I J J K K L L
M M N N O O P P
Q Q R R S S T T
U U V V W W X X
Y Y Z Z

65

Sit tall.
Keep both feet
on the floor.

Look at the picture.
Then look at the
way you hold your
pencil. Do not hold
your pencil too
tightly.

Slant your paper like this. Hold your
paper steady with your right hand.

Slant your paper like this.
Hold your paper steady
with your left hand.

Sit tall.
Keep both feet
on the floor.

Look at the picture.
Then look at the
way you hold your
pencil. Do not hold
your pencil too
tightly.

67

Matching Manuscript and Cursive Letters

Draw lines to match cursive and manuscript letters.

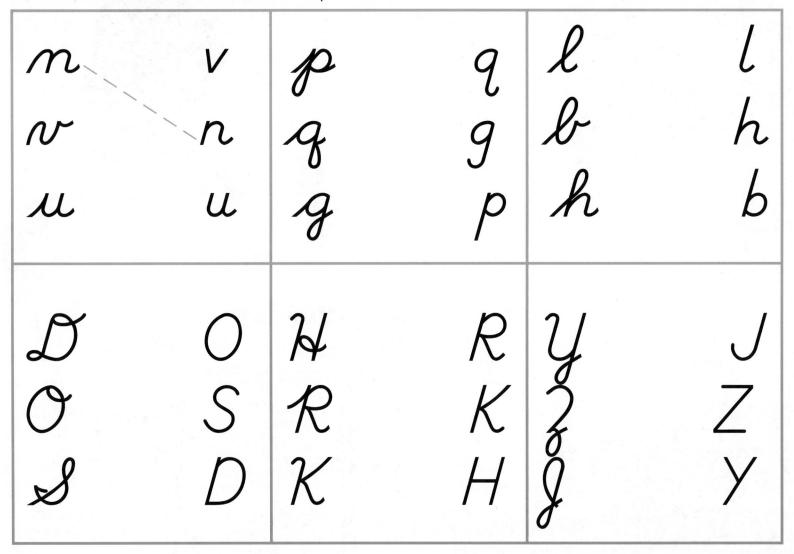

Matching Manuscript and Cursive Words

Read the word in the box. Circle the word that matches it.

bear	hear	bear	dear
went	went	west	want
fan	far	pan	fan
skate	shake	skate	slate
meat	meat	meal	neat

Recognizing Cursive Letters

Read each cursive letter. Print the manuscript letter that matches it.

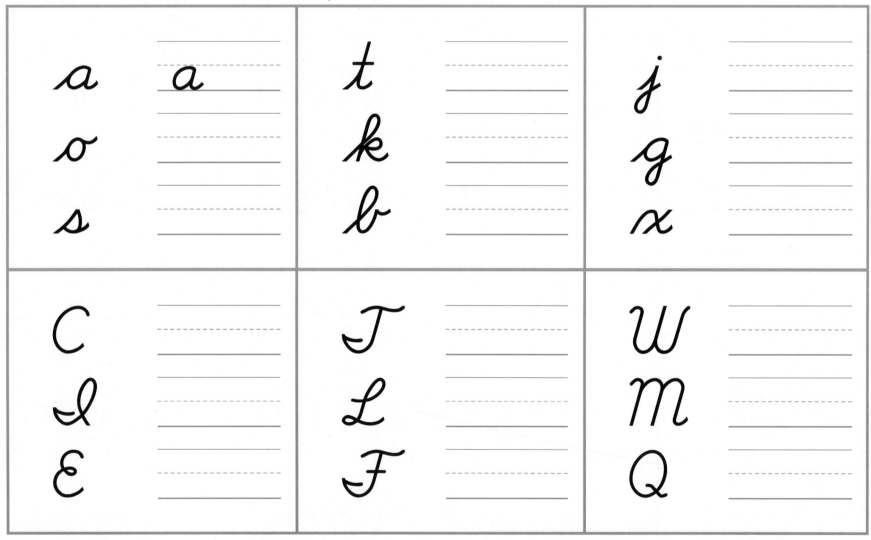

Recognizing Cursive Words

Read each cursive word. Print it in manuscript.

say   say

Carl

mop

buzz

have

quit

king

fox

jaw

Dee

Comparing Manuscript and Cursive Letters

Many manuscript and cursive letters look very much alike. Look at the letters below. Tell how each manuscript letter was changed to make a cursive letter.

Manuscript

h k l t a d m n

Cursive

h k l t a d m n

These manuscript and cursive letters do not look very much alike. Can you name the letters in the cursive row?

Manuscript

b f r s v z

Cursive

b f r s v z

Undercurve Connections

Many cursive letters begin with a stroke called an undercurve. An undercurve looks a little like an ocean wave.

Try making some undercurves. Notice that they can be short or tall.

When you add an undercurve to these manuscript letters, you make cursive letters.

e h i j k l p t u w y

Look at how undercurve letters connect.

h i l l hill k i t e kite

77

Overcurve Connections

Some cursive letters begin with a stroke called an overcurve.
An overcurve looks a little like part of a hill.

Practice making overcurves.

l l

When you add an overcurve to the beginning of these
manuscript letters, you make cursive letters.

a c d g m n o q v x

Look at how these overcurve letters connect.

c a n   can   a d d   add

Cross-Stroke Connections

Some letters **end** with a special stroke called a cross stroke. A cross stroke looks a little like a bridge.

Practice making cross strokes.

These letters end with a cross stroke.

b   o   v   w

When a cross stroke is used to connect two letters, the shape of the second letter changes. Look at how the letters change.

o   n   on   one   we   e   we   wet

Cursive writing slants.

Cursive writing slants.

All your letters should slant in the same direction.

The letters slant correctly.

Do not slant letters in different directions.
Your writing may not be easy to read.

What is wrong here?

Spacing in Cursive Writing

Leave the space of a pencil point between letters.

mouse

Leave the space of a pencil between words.

my dog

Leave a finger space between sentences.

What is that? It is a cat.

Space letters and words evenly. Your writing will look better if you do.

Correct spacing

his frog

Incorrect spacing

her fish

Read each cursive word. Print it in manuscript.

how

Ann

sit

Mel

Tell which words slant correctly.

mice

hill

went

late

said

bend

Tell which words have letters that are spaced correctly.

about   many   read   little

Book Report
Circus Life by Ima Clown
is about circus clowns. It
tells how clowns get ready
for circuses.

i i

i

i _ _ _ _ _ _ _ i _ _ _ _ _ _ _ i

i _ _ _ _ _ _ _ i _ _ _ _ _ _ _ i

i _ _ _ _ _ _ _ i _ _ _ _ _ _ _ i

ii i i ii

ii

80   **SELF CHECK**   Circle your best *i*.

t t

t l t

t

t   t   t

t   t   t

t   t   t

tt t t tt

it i t it

★ **ON YOUR OWN**   Draw a picture of your favorite circus animal.

u u

u

u _____ u _____ u

u _____ u _____ u

ut u t ut

tu t u tu

tutu tutu

82 **ON YOUR OWN** Write two words that tell about clowns.

s s

s s s

s

s _ _ _ _ _ _ _ s _ _ _ _ _ s

s _ _ _ _ _ _ _ s _ _ _ _ _ s

ss s s ss

si s i si

su s u su

sit sit

suit suit

⭐ **ASK A FRIEND**   Have a friend circle an *s* that slants correctly.

83

e *e*

e

e

e _ _ _ _ _ _ _ *e* _ _ _ _ *e*

e _ _ _ _ _ _ _ *e* _ _ _ _ *e*

ee *e* *e* *ee*

se *s* *e* *se*

see see

set set

use use

84 **ASK A FRIEND** Have a friend circle any *e* that looks like an uncrossed *t*.

l l   l

l

l   l   l

l   l   l

ll l l ll

li l i li

little little

tilt tilt

stilts stilts

ON YOUR OWN What's the most amazing thing you might see at a circus? Draw an amazing circus scene.

r _ _ _ _ _ _ _ _ _ _ _ _ _ r

r _ _ _ _ _ _ _ _ _ _ _ _ _ r

r _ _ _ _ _ _ _ _ _ _ _ _ _ r

ri ri rise rise

tr tr tries tries

rise

tries

true

86　**SELF CHECK**　Circle the word you wrote best.

C c

c

c _ _ _ _ _ _ _ _ _ c _ _ _ _ _ _ c

c _ _ _ _ _ _ _ _ _ c _ _ _ _ _ _ c

ci ci   circus circus

cl cl   circle circle

circus circle

⭐ **ON YOUR OWN**   Make up a riddle about a circus animal. Have a friend answer your riddle.

87

a a

a

a _ _ _ _ _ a _ _ _ _ a

a _ _ _ _ _ a _ _ _ _ a

al al   all all

ar ar   star star

ea ea   seal seal

a seal act

SPANKY

ASK A FRIEND   Have a friend circle your best a.

d d

d d d

d

d _____ d _____ d

d _____ d _____ d

di di   did did

de de   ride ride

ad ad   add add

rider rides

ON YOUR OWN   The horses whinny. The elephants trumpet.
Make a circus sound or describe one to a partner.

Linking Handwriting to Writing

Writing a Word Web

Copy the circus word web.

circus

stars

acts

stilts

seals

ON YOUR OWN Think of more circus words to add to the word web.

Copy these phrases. Remember to use your best cursive handwriting.

true circus stars
real creatures
still a success

Circle a word you spaced correctly.

Circle a word in which all the letters slant correctly.

91

o o

o o o

o

o _ _ _ _ _ _ _ o _ _ _ _ _ o

o _ _ _ _ _ _ _ o _ _ _ _ _ o

oo o o o oo   toot

recorder

solo

SELF CHECK   Circle your best o .

g g g

g

g _ _ _ _ _ _ g _ _ _ _ _ _ g

g _ _ _ _ _ _ g _ _ _ _ _ _ g

guitar guitar

la guitarra

guitar guide

ON YOUR OWN

How do you feel when you're listening to your favorite music?
Share your feelings with a partner.

m m

1 m 2 m 3 m

m

m _____ _____ m _____ _____ m

m _____ _____ m _____ _____ m

music music

om o m om

some more music

ON YOUR OWN

Roll modeling clay into long, thin strips. Use the strips of clay
to form the cursive letter m.

n m

m n n

m

m _ _ _ _ _ m _ _ _ _ _ m

m _ _ _ _ _ m _ _ _ _ _ m

notes notes

un u n un   tune

notes in a song

ASK A FRIEND   Have a friend circle any *n*'s that do not have rounded tops.

Linking Handwriting to Writing

Writing to Add Details

Proofreading The box shows proofreading marks you can use to correct mistakes or to add more details.

Notice how proofreading marks are used with these details about a song.

Proofreading Marks	
∧	Add words.
—	Take out words.

a ~~a~~ song

^{comical}
a ∧ song

^{long,}
a ∧ comical song

^{loud,}
a ∧ long, comical song

96 **COMPUTER TIP** Look closely at a computer keyboard. Find the key that helps you delete, or take out, letters or words. Find the key that helps you insert, or put in, letters or words.

Final Draft   Copy the details about a song from the previous page. Make the corrections that the proofreading marks show.

HANDWRITING TIP   Remember to connect the letters of the words.

 ON YOUR OWN   If you wrote a loud, long, comical song, what would it be about? Write a title for your song and share it with a classmate.

h h

h h

h

h _ _ _ _ _ h _ _ _ _ _ h

h _ _ _ _ _ h _ _ _ _ _ h

hear hear

hoot hoot

hearing hoots

SELF CHECK Circle a word you spaced correctly.

k k   1 k   k   3 k   k

k   k   k
k   k   k

knock knock

tick tick

ticktock clock

ON YOUR OWN   List things that make knocking or ticking sounds.

j j

j   *j*   *j*

j

j — — — — *j* — — — *j*

j — — — — *j* — — — *j*

jingle jingle

jiggle to jingle

⭐ **ON YOUR OWN**   Use string and metal washers to make jiggly, jingly instruments.

y y   y y²

y

y ___ y ___ y

y ___ y ___ y

yell yell

noisy noisy

youngsters yelling

ASK A FRIEND   Have a friend circle your best y.

Linking Handwriting to Writing

Writing a Learning Log

Copy the information in the learning log below.

animal sounds

cluck, roar, moo, hiss,

rustle, coo, oink

102 ⭐ **ON YOUR OWN** Think about your favorite sound. Discuss with an adult what causes that sound.

Copy these phrases. Remember to use your best cursive handwriting.

hum, honk, hush

chatter, cluck, knock

creaky, crunchy, jingle

Circle a word you spaced correctly.

Circle a word in which all the letters slant correctly.

P P

p *p* *p*

p

p — — — — — — *p* — — — — — — *p*

p — — — — — — *p* — — — — — — *p*

picture picture

special step

proud person

SELF CHECK Circle a word in which all the letters slant correctly.

b b

b b b

b

b   b   b

b   b   b

bi b i bi   big

a big job

broad boulder

ON YOUR OWN Describe to a partner what you think the moon looks like.
Have your partner draw a picture to fit your description.

W w w

¹ *w* ² *w* ³ *w* ⁴ *w*

w

w _____ _____ *w* _____ _____ *w*

w _____ _____ *w* _____ _____ *w*

wh   w   h   wh   where

who knows where

whose shadow

★ ON YOUR OWN   Dip a paintbrush tip into water. Use the paintbrush to
practice writing *w*'s on a chalkboard.

$f\ f$

f 1 f 2 f 3 f

f

f f f

f f f

flag flag   fine feeling

faraway flag

ASK A FRIEND   Have a friend circle your best f.

Writing a Book Report

To Space and Back
by Sally Ride and Susan Okie

The book I read is about

astronauts in outer space.

From this book, I learned

you can float from one place to another.

This book made me want to

go to the moon.

Copy the book report.

To Space and Back
by Sally Ride and Susan Okie

This book is about

From this book, I learned

This book made me want to

ON YOUR OWN   Read the report to a friend.

q q

q q q

q

q — — — — q — — — q

q — — — — q — — — q

quart quart

a quart of liquid

some questions

110 SELF CHECK Circle a word that is spaced correctly.

x x

x

x ———— x ———— x

x ———— x ———— x

mix mix

exploring matter

next experiment

ON YOUR OWN Half fill a clear glass with water. Blow into the water with a straw. Write about what happens.

111

v V v

v

v _ _ _ _ _ _ *v* _ _ _ _ _ *v*

v _ _ _ _ _ _ *v* _ _ _ _ _ *v*

visible visible

invisible gas

moving air

ON YOUR OWN Try to blow a crayon and a feather from your desktop. Tell which object is easier to move.

Z z

z

z z z

z z z

zero zero

frozen solid

a great size

⭐ **ASK A FRIEND** Have a friend circle your best word.

Writing Science Notes

Copy the information in the notes below.

solids take up space	liquids flow	gases usually unseen

solids	liquids	gases

ON YOUR OWN Use your index finger to write words on a tray covered with sand.

Stone Soup

Begin with a stone. What would you add to the pot to make a delicious soup? Write your own recipe for your soup.

Copy these phrases. Remember to use
your best cursive handwriting.

fizzing liquid

answers to big questions

everything explained

Circle a word you
spaced correctly.

Circle a word in
which all the letters
slant correctly.

UNIT 6

Writing to Celebrate

It's a Party!

Date: July 14

Time: 12 noon

Place: Meet at Mark's. We're going to a ball game!

A a   a   a   a

a _____ a _____ a

a _____ a _____ a

April 10 is the birthday
of Andy Adam Ames.

ON YOUR OWN   Find out the next birthday in your family. Circle the date
on a calendar to help you remember that special date.

C C C

C

C   C   C

C   C   C

Carla mailed invitations.

Come and celebrate!

Bill Smith
270

Erin Evans
555 Cutter Lane
West Covina, CA 91713

SELF CHECK Circle your best C.

119

E Ɛ

Ɛ¹ Ɛ²

Ɛ

Ɛ   Ɛ   Ɛ

Ɛ   Ɛ   Ɛ

Erin's invitation

la invitación de Erin

A Birthday Party!
Andy Ames
April 10 at 1 o'clock
321 River Road

ASK A FRIEND   Have a friend circle any Ɛ's that need improvement because they do not loop at the midline.

120

OO

O

O   O   O

O   O   O

Owen will go too.

Owen asistirá también.

9

10
Andy's Party

17

⭐ ON YOUR OWN   List some decorations you might use at a birthday party.

Q Q

Q

Q   Q   Q

Q   Q   Q

Quinn and Qiana
chose a birthday gift.

SELF CHECK Circle your best Q.

B B

B B B

B

B   B   B

B   B   B

Ben is wrapping the gift.

Be careful, Ben.

ON YOUR OWN Make your own special wrapping paper. Decorate the paper with the initials of the person who will receive the gift.

123

P P

1 P 2 P

P

P — — — P — — — P

P — — — P — — — P

Perry will bring
a Punchy Pal.

124 **ASK A FRIEND** Have a friend circle your best P.

R R

R R R

R

R   R   R

R   R   R

Roxy will bring her
Rita Reptile video.

RITA
REPTILE

⭐ ON YOUR OWN

Write two sentences about your favorite video. Tell the title of the video and why you like watching it.

H H

Here is a card.

Happy Birthday!

Have fun!

ON YOUR OWN Make a birthday card with a special message for a friend or family member.

K K

K *K* *K*

K

K _____ *K* _____ *K*

K _____ *K* _____ *K*

Keep playing games.

Andy's party is OK!

SELF CHECK Circle a word you wrote smoothly.

Using Punctuation

The Comma

Use a comma in dates. It separates the day from the year.

April 5, 1995

Use a comma in addresses. It separates the city from the state.

Oahu, Hawaii

Sometimes you list three or more things in a sentence. Use a comma to separate the things.

Here are my toys, games, and books.

ON YOUR OWN Look in a book to find a place where commas are used. Copy the sentence.

The Exclamation Point

A sentence that shows a strong feeling is an **exclamation.**
Use an exclamation point at the end of an exclamation.

! ─ ─ ─ ─ ─ ─ ─ ! ─ ─ ─ ─ ─ ─ !

A birthday is today!

Balloons are everywhere!

Come on! Open the gifts!

ON YOUR OWN   Draw a birthday balloon with a special message on it. Use an exclamation point.

129

Writing an Invitation

Proofreading The box shows proofreading marks you can use to correct mistakes.

Use the marks to change three lowercase letters that should be capitals and one capital that should be lowercase.

Proofreading Marks		
≡	Use a capital letter.	karen
/	Change a capital letter to lowercase.	In

A Birthday Party!

Andy ames

April 10 At 1 o'clock

321 river road

⌨ **COMPUTER TIP** Find the key on the computer keyboard that helps you make capital letters.

Final Draft   Copy the invitation from the previous page.
Make the corrections that the proofreading marks show.

HANDWRITING TIP   Remember to leave a space as wide
as a pencil between words.

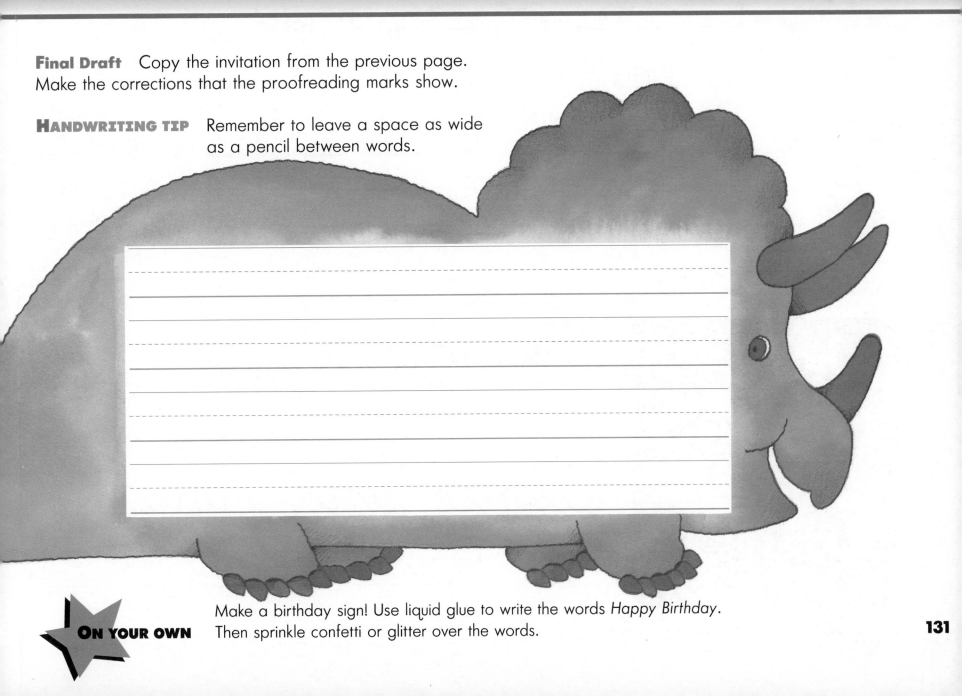

Make a birthday sign! Use liquid glue to write the words *Happy Birthday.*
Then sprinkle confetti or glitter over the words.

ON YOUR OWN

131

$\mathcal{D}$ $\mathcal{D}$

$\mathcal{D}$

$\mathcal{D}$ $\mathcal{D}$ $\mathcal{D}$

$\mathcal{D}$ $\mathcal{D}$ $\mathcal{D}$

Dancers!

Decorate today.

Dance and sing.

132   **ON YOUR OWN**   Look up information about Cinco de Mayo to share with classmates.

T T

T   T

T

T   T   T

T   T   T

The music fills the park.

Today is special.

F F

F

F   F   F

F   F   F

Feel the excitement!

Fiesta!

ASK A FRIEND   Ask a friend to circle any F that isn't crossed.

I I

I I

I I

Imagine you are there.

It's lively.

ON YOUR OWN Imagine there will be a big party soon in your neighborhood. Make a colorful poster that invites neighbors to the party.

G G

G

G _ _ _ _ _ _ _ *G* _ _ _ _ _ _ *G*

G _ _ _ _ _ _ _ *G* _ _ _ _ _ _ *G*

Groups gather to hear.

Get ready.

SELF CHECK Circle a *G* you wrote smoothly.

S S

S

S

S

S

S

Shush!

Stop and listen.

Sweet music plays.

ON YOUR OWN What is your favorite musical instrument? Write a paragraph to describe it.

MM m

m m m m

m _ _ _ _ _ _ _ m _ _ _ _ _ m

m _ _ _ _ _ _ m _ _ _ _ _ m

Cinco de Mayo is here.

May 5

138 SELF CHECK Circle your best m.

N n

n n n

n   n   n

n   n   n

Neighbors come together.

New friends share.

⭐ **ON YOUR OWN** How does your family or neighborhood celebrate a holiday?
Write a paragraph to describe the celebration.

Linking Handwriting to Writing

Writing a Thank-You Note

Copy the thank-you note on your paper. Do not copy the words in blue.

Heading *May 8, 1994*

Greeting *Dear Teresa,*

Body *Thank you for taking me to the fiesta. I really had fun.*

Closing *Gracias,*

Signature *Sara*

ON YOUR OWN Write a thank-you note to someone who has done something you appreciate.

Copy these sentences. Remember to use your best cursive handwriting.

Hey! I hear music.
A fiesta is starting.
Put on a costume.
Diego will bring Chiang.

Circle the letter you wrote best.

Circle a word you wrote smoothly.

J *J*

J   *J*   *J*   *J*

J   *J*   *J*

J   *J*   *J*

Jin is on the team.

Jeri plays too.

SELF CHECK   Circle your best *J*.

L L

L L L

L

L _ _ _ _ L _ _ _ _ L

L _ _ _ _ L _ _ _ _ L

Left field is
Libby's spot.

Let's play!

★ **ON YOUR OWN**   Write a few sentences to tell what you like about your favorite sport.

143

$\mathcal{U}\ \mathcal{U}$

$\mathcal{U}\ \mathcal{U}$

$\mathcal{U}$

$\mathcal{U}$ _ _ _ _ _ _ $\mathcal{U}$ _ _ _ _ _ $\mathcal{U}$

$\mathcal{U}$ _ _ _ _ _ _ $\mathcal{U}$ _ _ _ _ _ $\mathcal{U}$

Umpire Upton signals.

Ursula is safe!

144 **ASK A FRIEND** Have a friend circle any $\mathcal{U}$ that needs improvement because it doesn't end just above the baseline.

V U

U

U   U   U

U   U   U

Vince hit a home run.

The Volcanoes win!

Victory!

ON YOUR OWN   Imagine you are a reporter. Interview a partner who pretends to be a sports star.

𝒲𝒲 ¹↷𝒰 ²↓𝒰 𝒰

𝒲 __ __ 𝒲 __ __ 𝒲

𝒲 __ __ 𝒲 __ __ 𝒲

We win! We win!

We're number one!

Wow!

SELF CHECK Circle a 𝒲 you wrote smoothly.

X X

X

X   X   X

X   X   X

Xavier cheers.

Coach Xin laughs.

ON YOUR OWN   Use long pieces of colorful yarn to form X's.

147

Y Y

Y Y Y

Y

Y   Y   Y

Y   Y   Y

Yes, let's celebrate.

You can come, Yuri.

ASK A FRIEND Have a friend circle your best Y.

Z z

We beat the Zane zebras.

Zak took pictures.

ON YOUR OWN   Write a cheer for a favorite sports team. Tape-record your cheer with some classmates.

Read the letter.

Heading

July 6, 1994

Greeting

Dear Grandpa,

Body

Boy, did you miss a big game! I hit a home run for you.

Closing

Love,

Signature

Vince

Copy the letter that is on page 150. Do not copy the words in blue.

Think of someone who missed one of your very happy times. Share that time by sending a friendly letter and a photograph or drawing to that person.

The address on an envelope shows where the letter goes. Every address has the following.

1. The name of the person getting the letter
2. The number of the house and the name of the street
3. The city, the state, and the ZIP code

Copy the address on your paper.

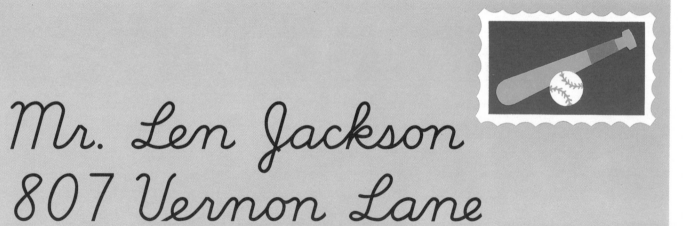

Mr. Len Jackson
807 Vernon Lane
Toledo, OH 43624

ON YOUR OWN Write the name and address of someone you would like to send a letter to, or write your own name and address.

You probably have a special way of tossing a ball. First, you learned the correct way to toss a ball. Next, you practiced it until you could do it easily. Then, you discovered you could toss a ball in a way that was both correct and all your own. You could do it by using your **personal style**.

You can use your personal style in handwriting too. Look closely at the words below. Notice the sizes of the letters in the first row and the slant of the letters in the next row.

wide narrow

right left straight

Use your personal style to write the word *pitcher.*

Copy these sentences. Remember to use your best cursive handwriting.

Join the Volcanoes.
Whip the Zebras.
Lin is out! Unfair!
Yea! Xenon has a hit!

Circle the capital letter you wrote best.

Circle a word you wrote smoothly.

On your own paper, copy the poem "Writing on the Chalkboard"
by Isabel Joshlin Glaser. Begin with the title. Use your best **cursive**
handwriting.

Writing on the Chalkboard
Up and down, my chalk goes.
Squeak, squeak, squeak!
Hush, chalk.
Don't squawk.
Talk softly when you speak.